PROPAGATING
FRUIT PLANTS

Copyright © C. Thornton 2013

The right of C. Thornton to be identified as creator of this work has been asserted in accordance with the Copyright, Designs and Patents Act, 1988.

All rights reserved. No part of this book may be reproduced or transmitted by any person or entity (including Google, Amazon or similar organisations) in any form or by any means, electronic or mechanical, including photocopying, recording or by any information storage and retrieval system, without prior permission in writing from the publisher.

National Library of Australia Cataloguing-in-Publication entry

Author: Thornton, C., author.

Title: Propagating fruit plants / C. Thornton, David Alexander Crichton.

ISBN: 9781925110517 (paperback)

Series: Rare and heritage fruit ; Set 2, no. 1.

Notes: Includes bibliographical references and index.

Subjects: Plant propagation.
Fruit trees--Propagation--Australia.
Fruit trees--Heirloom varieties.

Other Authors/Contributors:
Crichton, David Alexander, author.

Dewey Number: 634.043

ABN 67 099 575 078
PO Box 9113, Brighton, 3186, Victoria, Australia
www.leavesofgoldpress.com

RARE AND HERITAGE FRUIT
GROWING #1

PROPAGATING FRUIT PLANTS

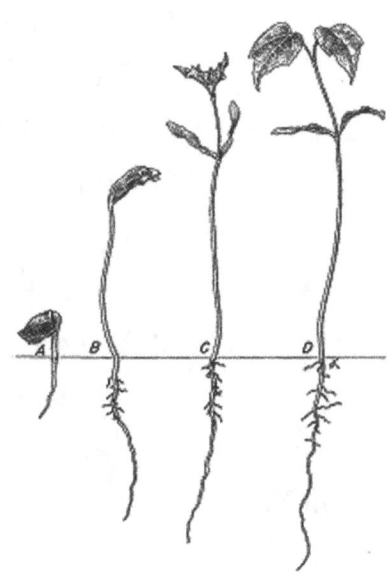

C. Thornton and David Alexander Crichton

- RARE AND HERITAGE FRUIT -
THE SERIES

SET #1
RARE AND HERITAGE FRUIT
- CULTIVARS -

1 Apples
2 Cider Apples
3 Crabapples
4 European Pears
5 Nashi Pears
6 Perry Pears
7 Apricots
8 Peaches
9 Nectarines
10 European Plums
11 Japanese Plums
12 Cherries
13 Figs
14 Cactus & Dragon Fruits
15 Oranges
16 Lemons
17 Limes
18 Mandarins & Grapefruit
19 Kumquats, Calamondins & Chinottos
20 Rare & Unusual Citrus
21 Nuts
22 Berries & Small Fruits
23 Quinces
24 Guavas & Feijoas
25 Table Grapes
26 Wine Grapes
27 Avocados
28 Rare & Unusual Fruits

and more...

SET #2
RARE AND HERITAGE FRUIT
- GROWING -

1 Propagating Fruit Plants (other than grafting)
2 Grafting and Budding Fruit Trees
3 Planting Fruit Trees and Shrubs
4 Care of Fruit Trees (compost, mulch, water etc)
5 Pruning Fruit Trees and Shrubs
6 Training and Espaliering Fruit Trees and Shrubs
7 Harvesting and Storage of Fruit
8 Pests and Diseases of Fruit Trees and Shrubs

SET #3
RARE AND HERITAGE FRUIT
- PRESERVING -

1 Fruit Preserving (drying, crystallizing, bottling etc.)
2 Cider Making
3 Perry Making ('pear cider')
4 Fruit Wine Making
5 Fruit Spirits and Liqueurs Making
6 Fruit Schnapps Making

www.leavesofgoldpress.com

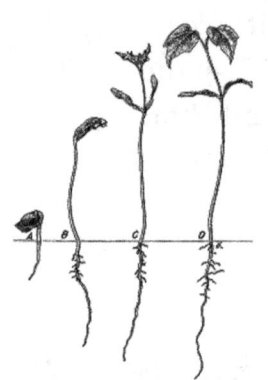

ABOUT RARE AND HERITAGE FRUIT[1]

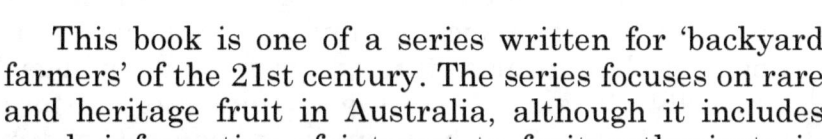

This book is one of a series written for 'backyard farmers' of the 21st century. The series focuses on rare and heritage fruit in Australia, although it includes much information of interest to fruit enthusiasts in every country.

For the purpose of this series, rare fruits are species neither indigenous to nor commercially cultivated in any given region.

'Heritage' or 'heirloom' fruits such as old-fashioned varieties[2] of apple, quince, fig, plum, peach and pear are increasingly popular due to their diverse flavours, excellent nutritional qualities and other desirable characteristics.

It is much easier for modern supermarkets to offer only a limited range of fruit cultivars (i.e. varieties) to consumers, instead of dozens of different kinds of apples, pears etc. During the 19th and early 20th centuries, however, the diversity was huge. Old

---

1   Note: this introduction is identical in every handbook in the Rare and Heritage Fruit series.

2   The correct term in this case is 'cultivars'; however most people are more familiar with the term 'varieties' and although it is not strictly accurate, we use the terms interchangeably in this series.

nursery catalogues were filled with numerous named varieties of fruits, nuts and berries, few of which are available these days.

What are heritage fruits? 'An heirloom plant, heirloom variety, heritage fruit (Australia), or (especially in the UK) heirloom vegetable is an old cultivar that is "still maintained by gardeners and farmers particularly in isolated or ethnic communities".[3]

'These may have been commonly grown during earlier periods in human history, but are not used in modern large-scale agriculture. Many heirloom vegetables have kept their traits through open pollination, while fruit varieties such as apples have been propagated over the centuries through grafts and cuttings.'[4]

Broadly speaking, heritage fruits are historic cultivars; those which have initially been selected or bred by human beings and given officially recognised names, before being propagated by successive generations of growers, retaining their genetic integrity far beyond the normal life-span of an individual plant; those which are not protected by a private plant-breeders' licence, but instead belong to the public at large. They are the legacy of our ancestors; living heirlooms; part of humanity's horticultural, vintage and culinary heritage.

Fruit enthusiasts around the globe are currently reviving our horticultural legacy by renovating old orchards and identifying rare, historic fruit varieties. The goal is to make a much wider range of fruit trees available again to the home gardener.

This series of handbooks aims to help.

---

3   Whealy, K. (1990). "Seed Savers Exchange: preserving our genetic heritage".(*Transactions of the Illinois State Horticultural Society 123: 80–84.)*
4   *'Heirloom plants'* Wikipedia, accessed October 2013

STORIES

Like people, every fruit cultivar has a name and a story. Take the Granny Smith apple, for example - the most successful Australian apple, instantly identifiable with its smooth green skin, exported world-wide, and now cultivated in numerous countries.

This famous cultivar began in the 1860s as a tiny seedling that chanced to spring up in a compost heap. An orchardist by the name of Mrs Maria Ann Smith lived with her ailing husband in Eastwood, New South Wales (now a suburb of Sydney). She was in her late sixties, a hard worker and the mother of many children.

One autumn day, as usual, Maria Smith drove her horse-drawn wagon home from the Sydney markets, where she had been selling the fruit from her orchard. The wagon possibly contained a few wooden crates she had purchased after selling her produce, in which to transport the next load of wares. One or two leftover Tasmanian-grown French Crab apples might still have been lying in the crates, somewhat battered and past their prime. Imagine 'Granny' Smith, her grey hair tucked up inside her bonnet, trudging down to the creek from which the household drew its water and dumping their decaying remains on its banks.

There in that damp spot, sinking into compost-rich soil, the apple pips lay throughout the winter months. Come spring, one of them split open and a tiny white rootlet appeared. It swiftly bored downwards, stood up and threw off its black seed-case, revealing two perfect, green cotyledons.

The leaves quickly multiplied as the seedling grew, Maria spied it next time she walked down to the creek, the hems of her long black skirts rustling through the ferns. She nurtured the infant tree until it grew up and bore fruit. When at last she picked the first green-skinned apple and took a bite, she must have been surprised by the crisp, hard flesh and sharp taste. No doubt she used it to make pies and other desserts for her sick husband and numerous grand-children, thus discovering that this new cultivar was good for both cooking and eating.

She shared the apples with friends and neighbours, allowing them to cut scion-wood from her tree and graft their own cloned versions. Locally, word of the apple's qualities spread.

'Smith died only a couple years after her discovery, but dozens of Granny Smith apple trees lived on in her neighbours' orchards. Her new cultivar did not receive widespread attention until, in 1890, it was exhibited as 'Smith's Seedling' at the Castle Hill Agricultural and Horticultural Show. The following year it won the prize for cooking apples under the name 'Granny Smith's Seedling'.

'The apple became a hit. In 1895 the New South Wales Department of Agriculture officially recognized the cultivar and began growing it at the Government Experimental Station in Bathurst, New South Wales, recommending its properties as a late-picking cooking apple for potential export.

'During the first half of the 20th century the government actively promoted the apple, leading to its widespread acceptance. However, its worldwide fame grew from the fact that it was such a good 'keeper'. Because of its excellent shelf life the Granny Smith could be transported over long distances in cold storage and in most seasons. Granny Smiths were exported in enormous quantities after the First World War, and by 1975 forty percent of Australia's apple crop was Granny Smiths. By this time the apple was being grown extensively elsewhere in the southern hemisphere, as well as in France, Great Britain and the United States.'

'The advent of the Granny Smith Apple is now celebrated annually in Eastwood with the Granny Smith Festival.[5]

Fruit cultivar stories continue to arise in the 21st century. From AAP, February 21, 2010, 'Mudgee Farmer Bruce Davis Creates New Fruit':

'Is it a plum? Is it a peach? It's probably a pleach as it's a morph of the two tasty stone fruits. Whatever it is, it's a love child of the two, accidentally created by a retired NSW farmer.

'Bruce Davis from Mudgee in the state's central west couldn't believe it when he discovered he had grown a cross between a peach and a plum. The fruit looks like a peach from the outside, but resembles a red plum when bitten into. 'The unusual fruit is believed to be the first of its kind ever grown in the state.

'Mr Davis grows peach and blood plum trees alongside each other and believes the peach/plum tree may have grown from compost that contained plum seeds.

'"It's a really interesting piece of fruit and it's very tasty," Mr Davis said.

'A cross between a plum and an apricot, known as a pluot, has been grown in the past, but a peach and a plum is a new combination for NSW, Primary Industries Minister Steve Whan said.

'Industry and Investment NSW Mudgee horticulturist Susan Marte said this was the first time she had heard of anyone accidentally crossing the two fruits.'

---

5   *'Granny Smith Festival'. Wikipedia, accessed October 2013*

NAMES

The origins of the Mudgee pleach and the Granny Smith apple are two of many intriguing fruit stories, but sometimes the name - or names - of cultivars tells yet another story, an etymological one. Names may be inspired by the place a new cultivar was discovered, by the person who selected or bred it, by the shape, flavour, colour or use of the fruit, by an event that took place around the time of discovery, by somebody's sweetheart, or any number of other factors.

Names, too, may be multiplied.

The Granny Smith apple was discovered after the advent of newspapers. If you forgot what the prize-winning cultivar was called, you could look it up and there it would be, in black and white. This was not the case for many ancient cultivars.

The Granny Smith apple's probable mother, the French Crab, itself boasts twenty-six listed synonyms, probably invented by forgetful apple-growers.

Another instance of numerous synonyms is the French cider apple whose name is Calville Rouge D'Hiver, meaning 'Calville Winter Red'. It arose in the late 1500s, and as its popularity spread across Europe, the first thing that happened was that people translated the name into their own language: 'Teli Piros Kalvil', 'Roter Winter Calville, 'Calvilla Rossa di Pasqua', 'Cerveny Zimni Hranac' etc.

Next, when absent-minded peasants could not remember the name of this excellent red fruit, they gave it another one. Imagine a weather-beaten farmer in some isolated French village scratching his beard and musing, 'It was something to do with "Calville". 'Calville Rouge,' perchance?' Across the valley in another village, a cider-brewer was knitting his (or her) puzzled brow and saying, 'It was something to do with winter, I am thinking, or was it autumn? "Pomme d'Automne"?' Further afield, a third Frenchman shrugged his shoulders and declared, 'Devil take me if I can remember how it is called, but it is big and red like the heart of a bull, so let us name it '"Coeur de Boeuf."'

Fanciful, perhaps, but this might explain why, on the database of the UK's National Fruit Collection, there are more than a hundred synonyms listed for Calville Rouge D'Hiver.

Words are forever evolving. Even when cultivar names stay the same, the language around them is changing and their original meaning becomes lost in the mists of time.

One example of this is the grape cultivar Cabernet Sauvignon, which is considered a relatively new variety, being the product of a chance 17th century crossing between Cabernet franc and Sauvignon blanc.

'Cabernet franc' can be etymologically traced back to 'French Black Grape' (from the Latin word 'caput' which means 'black vine'). The word 'Sauvignon' is believed to be derived from the French 'sauvage', meaning 'wild' and to refer to the grape being a wild grapevine native to France. 'Blanc,' of course, means 'white'. 'Cabernet Sauvignon' no longer means 'Wild Black Grape' in modern French - that would translate as something like 'Vigne Noir Sauvage'. The ancient cultivar name has now taken on its own meaning and is virtually synonymous with the wine made from it.

It is interesting to compare typical cider apple names with, say, typical peach or perry pear names. French words abound among heritage cider apple cultivars, reflecting their roots in medieval Normandy. To the ears of English-speakers these names may sound rather mysterious and aristocratic, until you translate them: for example, Gros Bois, Jaune de Vitré, Moulin à Vent du Calvados, Noël des Champs, Belle Fille de la Manche, Petite Sorte du Parc Dufour and Groin D'âne translate respectively as Big Wood, Yellow Glass, Windmill of Calvados, Christmas Field, Beautiful Girl of the English Channel, Small Kind of Park of the Oven and Donkey's Groin.

Some names of heritage perry pears give us an insight into the bawdy, rustic humour of the perry-drinking English peasants who originally selected them; Ram's Cods, Startle Cock and Bloody Bastard to mention a few.

Heritage grape cultivars have names that come from all over Europe, particularly France and Italy.

Figs go back even further. Humans were cultivating them around 9400 BC, a thousand years before wheat and rye were domesticated. Their names, in English at least, are often drawn from their colour and their place of origin - Brown Turkey, White Adriatic, Black Genoa, Pink Jerusalem, Green Ischia ...

Peaches, a more 'modern' fruit in terms of their popularity and breeding, often bear invented names with fancy spellings, such as Florda Glo, Earligrande, Harbrite and Dixigem.

'IMMORTAL' DNA

Another major difference between stone fruit and fruits such as grapes, figs and apples is their ability to grow 'true' to their parents from seed. Stone fruits are far more homozygous than their ancient cousins the pomes (apples, pears etc.) and the grapes. Growers do graft them, but if you plant their seeds the new tree will bear fruit that's fairly similar to that of the parent tree. This means that the centuries-old grafting traditions, the fierce cherishing, the careful bequeathing and the meticulous labelling that accompany pome fruits, grapes and other heterozygotes are not seen as often in the world of peaches and nectarines. This is why many of their cultivar names seem so different, arising as they do from highly organised commercial breeding programmes of the 20th and 21st centuries.

Unlike the seedlings of say, peaches and nectarines, seedling apples are an example of 'extreme heterozygotes', in that rather than inheriting DNA from their parents to create a new apple with those characteristics, they are instead significantly different from their parents.'[6] (Humans are rather like apples in that way, though not as extreme.)

Returning to our green-skinned Australian apple - 'Because the Granny Smith is a chance (and rare) mutation, its seeds tend to produce trees whose fruit have a much less appealing taste. To preserve the exact genetic code of any plant variety, a stick of the wood has to be 'cloned'. It has to be grafted onto new roots (or planted directly into the ground, but this is uncommon for trees). Thus, all the Granny Smith apple trees grown today are cuttings of cuttings of cuttings from the original Smith tree in Sydney.'[7]

Cloning by grafting means that the heritage trees - and shrubs - which have survived through the years are genetically identical to their ancestors. Indeed,

---

6 *John Lloyd and John Mitchinson (2006). QI: The Complete First Series – QI Factoids*
7 *Stirzaker, Richard (2010). Out of the Scientist's Garden: A Story of Water and Food. Collingwood, VIC: CSIRO Pub.*

the heritage plants of today possess exactly the same genetic code as the original trees that arose centuries ago in Asia and Europe. For example, another heritage apple cultivar, 'Court Pendu Plat', is thought to be 1500 years old - the oldest one in existence. Introduced into Europe during Roman times, the living wood from that same tree flourishes to this day, right here in the Great Southern Land.

RARE AND HERITAGE FRUIT IN AUSTRALIA

Many of the rare and heritage fruits that exist in Australia today are clonally descended from plants brought to our shores by the early European settlers, when few, if any, quarantine laws existed. Good luck rather than good stock monitoring limited the number of plant diseases unintentionally imported during the early days of colonization. Fortunately, by 1879 it was recognised that in order to prevent the introduction of serious pests and diseases, quarantine measures were needed. In 1908, the Commonwealth Quarantine service came into operation and took over local quarantine stations in every Australian state.

However, before 1879, there was no limit to the varieties of fruiting plants that could be imported into this country. Many of those old genetic lines survive to this day but sadly, many others have been lost.

Fortunately, Australia is one of only two countries free of fire blight, a serious and ineradicable disease that wiped out millions of apple, pear, loquat and quince trees in Europe and the USA during the 1900s. This means that when certain heritage cultivars went extinct elsewhere, they remained safe in this country. Some have now been restored to their region of origin, now grafted onto fire blight-resistant rootstock.

Over the course of the decades since 1879 Australian fruit growers imported (through quarantine) the latest new cultivars bred by overseas agricultural research stations. Year by year, as scientific advances in breeding and genetics were made, the older cultivars fell out of fashion and were swept aside in favour of the new. They, too, became part of our almost forgotten fruit inheritance.

COMMERCIAL CULTIVARS

Naturally, plant breeders strive to provide the products demanded by the market. Commercial orchardists want to purchase heavy-bearing trees with high disease resistance, whose fruit ripens all at the same time to save on picking costs. Wholesalers want fruit that keeps in storage for a long time without spoiling, and can be shipped without damage. Only firm-fleshed, bruise-resistant fruit will survive modern-day processing. After harvesting, apples, for instance, are tipped into crates, then passed along a conveyor belt through machinery that washes and brushes them clean of insecticides and dirt. This process removes some of the fruit's natural protective coating, so the machines re-apply a commercial grade wax before polishing them to a high shine and pasting a plastic label onto each one. Then the apples are packed into cartons for shipping to markets and stores.

Supermarket shoppers demand visually attractive fruit - large, regular in shape, unblemished and with highly coloured skin. Consumers also choose fruit with extra sugar content and juiciness.

All these characteristics, nonetheless, do not necessarily give rise to the best flavour or nutrition. To pick a tree-ripened fruit from your own back yard and bite into it is to experience the taste of fresh food as our forefathers knew it. Growing and preserving their own food, unconcerned with transportability and long storage times, they aimed for a wide variety of fruits, each of which had a unique and delicious taste.

Rare fruit, heritage and heirloom fruit enthusiasts across the world are reviving our horticultural legacy by renovating old orchards and sourcing 'lost' historic and unusual fruit varieties. Their goal is to encourage community participation and to make a wide range of fruit trees available again to the home gardener.

This series of handbooks aims to help.

WHY PRESERVE RARE AND HERITAGE FRUITS?

• They provide access to a wider range of unique and delicious flavours.
• We can enjoy the nutritional benefits of fresh, tree-ripened food.
• Biodiversity: The preservation of a wide range of vital genetic material helps to insure against the ravages of pests and diseases in the future.
• They allow a longer harvesting season, with early and late ripening.
• Culture: heritage varieties, with their interesting assortment of names, are living history.

Collections of heritage fruit trees are precious. Anyone who is the custodian of an old tree should treasure it.

CONTENTS

Introduction 1
Seeds 3
    True To Type 3
    How To Obtain Seeds 14
    How To Clean Seeds 14
    Seed Storage 15
    How To Prepare Seeds For Sowing 17
    Which Method For Which Seed? 36
Suckers 45
Layers 47
Cuttings 51
    Eye-cuttings 54
    Root-cuttings 56
Division 57
Bibliography 59
Glossary 61
Index 63

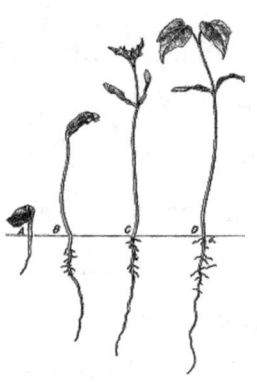

INTRODUCTION

This book outlines methods of propagating heritage fruits other than grafting, Grafting is covered in one of the other booklets in this series.

Covering such topics as propagation by seeds, suckers, layers, cuttings, eye-cuttings, root-cuttings and division, this book utilises the vast knowledge of 19th century writer David Alexander Crichton. Crichton was the official Australian government expert and lecturer upon 'Fruit Culture'. His work *The Australasian Fruit Culturist* (1893) is well worth reading, more than a century after it was published. The reader will be able to tell, by the differing styles of writing, which contributions have been made by Crichton.

While this book was written for Australian conditions, the basic principles of growing fruiting plants apply anywhere in the world.

The text has been edited and augmented to bring it up to date; however, propagation methods for the home gardener have changed relatively little over the years. Fruit trees respond to the same basic practices today as they did in the late 19th century.

Some diagrams from Plant Propagation (1922) by Walter Davis have been included.

SEEDS

'TRUE TO TYPE'

Most fruit seeds seldom produce a tree that is similar to the parent trees; they do not grow 'true to type'. That is one of the many reasons why fruit trees are usually propagated by grafting.

Take, for example, an apple. The seeds inside it (usually about 6 - 10) will all contain wildly different blends of the apple's parents' genes. The 6 -10 trees grown from those seeds, all from the same apple, will all look slightly different and bear fruit that looks and tastes different, not only from each other, but from the two parent trees, the mother tree (the one that bore the apple) and the father tree (the apple tree that gave its pollen).

You can plant a seed from a scrumptious apple and end up with a tree that bears bad-tasting fruit. You might also end up with the best-tasting apple in the world, but there's no way of knowing beforehand. It's a lottery.

Plants such as apples, which give rise to varying offspring, are known as 'heterozygotes', from 'hetero', meaning 'different' and 'zygote', meaning 'a fertilized ovum'. You could think of 'heterozygous' as meaning 'having kids that are different from the parents'. Heterozygous plants need to be cross pollinated to bear fruit. The mother tree's genes then mingle, in many different combinations, with the genes from the polleniser, creating hybrid offspring with different characteristics.

Apple rootstocks are normally propagated by layering, not by seed, because apple growers need certain valuable qualities to be passed on in their rootstocks - qualities such as disease resistance. Apple trees grown for their fruit are usually propagated by grafting.

Heterozygosity is an advantage for any plant or animal species. It gives that species a better chance of survival under uncertain and changeable conditions. With each new generation, individuals arise that are equipped to battle a wide range of adversities including drought, pestilence, flood etc.

FRUITS THAT GROW TRUE TO TYPE FROM SEED

There are, however, some fruits that grow 'true to type' from seed. Those that always turn out identical to their parents are called 'pure line' plants, and their genetic makeup is called 'homozygous' (from 'homo', meaning 'the same'). In other words, 'homozygous' means "having kids that are the same as the parents'. The plant's characteristics remain unchanged through succeeding generations. True to type plants that occur in nature are self fertile; that is, they produce fruit and seeds by fertilisation from their own pollen, not by using pollen from another plant.

There are, nonetheless, very many citrus fruits (and some mangoes) which almost always grow true to type from seed; whose offspring are essentially genetic clones of the parent.

'Most commercial [citrus] rootstock varieties produce mainly nucellar seedlings which do not inherit any of the traits of the "father" plant. This allows for the production of uniform rootstock, which yields consistent results in fruit production.

'Rootstocks such as 'Rough Lemon', 'Sour Orange', and 'Trifoliate orange' can be produced true-to-type from seed. This is important for nurseries because virus is not transmitted through either nucellar or zygotic seed. Thus, nurseries can produce virus-free, clonal rootstocks from seed.'[1]

'Most common citrus such as oranges, grapefruit, lemons and most mandarins are polyembryonic and will come true to type. The good news is that polyembryony helps stabilize varieties, which allows seeds to be passed around with little chance of spreading diseases such as viruses. This unique characteristic allows amateurs to grow citrus from seed, something you can't do with, say, apples.'[2]

A SPECTRUM

In between extreme heterozygosity on one hand and pure line homozygosity on the other, there exists a wide spectrum of zygosity. Some plants are more heterozygous than others. Apples and pears are extremely heterozygous, whereas stone fruits, for example, such as apricots and peaches, are only moderately so. Most peaches are self fertile, which is why the seedlings

---

1 *Citrus Pages, by Jorma Koskinen*
2 *'Hardy Citrus for the South East', by Tom McClendon. Southeastern Palm Society (SPS Publishing).*

have similar characteristics to the mother tree. They grow almost true to type.

'Open-pollinated plant varieties are produced from a population of 'parent' plants with very similar genetic characteristics. Open-pollinated plants, grown in isolation to prevent cross-pollination with another variety of the same species, will produce offspring that are very similar to the original parent population, allowing seeds to be saved and grown true to type year after year, generation after generation. For example, saved seed from a heritage 'Moon & Stars' watermelon (Citrullus lanatus) should produce another 'Moon & Stars' watermelon plant. Heirloom seeds are open-pollinated varieties that have been maintained and handed down by seed savers for at least 60 years.'[3]

If cross pollination occurs, the resulting seed will be a natural hybrid and may have some characteristics of each parent or may look completely different from either. So if by some chance your 'Moon & Stars' cross-pollinated with a nearby 'War Paint' watermelon, you will get some unusual watermelons from planting those seeds.[4]

GUARANTEEING TRUENESS TO TYPE

Aside from plants that produce nucellar seedlings, the only way you can guarantee that a new fruit tree or shrub will be identical to its parent is if that plant is grafted, layered, or grown from a cutting, offshoot or sucker.

---

3 *Frequently Asked Questions, Seeds of Change*
4 *Gardening, on About.com*

WHY PLANT FRUIT SEEDS?

Commercial peach growers use the pits (stones) from the previous year's canning crop to grow new rootstocks. Rootstocks grown from seed tend to be more vigorous and healthy than rootstocks grown by layering. This is because viruses are not transmitted through seeds; thus most seedlings are free from disease. Over the centuries, plant cultivars that have always been propagated by methods other than seed, (cuttings, layering, grafting etc.) build up a load of latent viruses in their tissue, which slows down their vigour.

'Stone fruit seedlings tend to have a deeper, more anchored root system than clonal rootstock, and have a lower probability of virus transmission from parent to progeny.'[5]

Another reason for planting fruit seeds is to create new hybrid cultivars - this is what plant breeders do.

One disadvantage of growing fruiting plants from seed is that it can take several years for the plant to become mature enough to bear fruit. Another is that their roots may not be resistant to some pests - for example, woolly aphid in apples.

If most fruits don't come true from seed, how can we use seeds to ensure the continuation of our heritage fruits?

1. We can sow seeds of fruits that are homozygous.

2. For those which are only partially homozygous, we can provide the best possible conditions for ensuring a pure line. One method is to grow open-pollinated seeds in isolation - as mentioned above - to keep similar varieties from cross-pollinating each

---

[5] *University of California Fruit and Nut Research*

other. This involves simply planting similar varieties far enough apart that their pollen cannot reach each other. Distance isolation requires no equipment or special skills, but it does rely on your having a good idea of who is growing what in your immediate area, which is not always possible.

Commercial seed growers also use other methods - they sow extensive plantings of the same variety. In very large plantings. Almost all undesired cross-pollination happens around the edges of the crop. The highest grades of certified genetically-pure seed are taken from the centres of large plantings, at specified distances from the edges. gardening.about.com

3. As for heterozygous plants, we simply cannot propagate them from seed and must use other methods, as outlined in this book.

If you have some space in your back yard, try growing fruit trees or fruiting shrubs from seed. You might plant a species that grows close to type, or you might want to take a gamble and see what grows from something extremely heterozygous, like an apple, a grape or a pear.

Many nurserymen disdain such practices, and will most likely assert that the trees and fruit will not be true-to-type and will therefore be of poor quality. However every new cultivar began life as a seedling, including the commercially successful plants they themselves sell! If your experiment fails, you can always use your tree as a rootstock.

A SELECTION OF FRUITS THAT GROW FAIRLY TRUE FROM SEED ...

... if self pollinated or pollinated by a closely similar cultivar.

Apricots (Prunus armeniaca)
Bayberry (Myrica spp.)
Berries, eg. Blackberry (Rubus fruticosus)
Brazilian Cherry/Surinam Cherry (Eugenia uniflora)
Ceylon Hill Gooseberry (Rhodomyrtus tomentosa)
Cherimoya/Custard Apple (Annona cherimola)
Cherry of the Rio Grande (Eugenia aggregate)
Damson Plum (Prunus domestica subsp. Insititia)
Dragon Fruit/Pitaya (Hylocereus spp. and Stenocereus spp.)
Feijoa (Acca sellowiana) Generally grown from seed and reproduces fairly, but not absolutely true to type.
Greengage Plum (Prunus italica)
Guavas (Psidium spp.)
Italian Stone Pine/Stone Pine (Pinus pinea)
Jaboticaba (Plinia cauliflora. Synonyms: Eugenia cauliflora, Eugenia jaboticaba, Myrcia jaboticaba, Myrciaria cauliflora, Myrciaria jaboticaba.) 'Species' jaboticabas grow true from seed.
Macadamia (Macadamia spp.) 'Species' macadamias grow true from seed.
Melons (Cucumis spp.) eg. Honeydew (Cucumis melo inodorus 'Honeydew')
Nectarines (Prunus persica var. nectarina)
Passionfruit (Passiflora edulis)
Peaches (Prunus persica)

Quince (Cydonia oblonga)
Saskatoon, Juneberry (Amelanchier spp.)
Sweet Chestnut ((Castanea sativa))
Tamarillo (Solanum betaceum) This grows fairly true from seed but is more easily propagated from cuttings.
Tomatillos (Physalis philadelphica), Cape gooseberries (Physalis peruviana), and ground cherries (Physalis pruinosa)
Tomato (Solanum lycopersicum) N.B. Tomatoes are really fruits.
Walnuts (Juglans nigra) grow somewhat true to seed.
Watermelons (Citrullus spp.) eg. Moon and Stars (Citrullus lanatus 'Moon and Stars'.)
Wild Strawberry (Fragaria vesca) This species strawberry is also called Woodland Strawberry, Alpine Strawberry, European strawberry, or Fraise des bois, and grows true from seed.

HIGHLY POLYEMBRYONIC CITRUS TYPES ...

... will mostly produce seeds that will grow true to type.

Citrus × aurantiifolia; Mexican Lime (Key Lime, West Indian Lime)
Citrus × insitorum (×Citroncirus webberii) Citranges, such as Rusk, Troyer etc.
Citrus × jambhiri 'Rough Lemon', 'Rangpur Lime', 'Otaheite Lime'
Citrus × limettioides, Palestine Lime (Indian Sweet Lime)
Citrus × microcarpa, 'Calamondin'
Citrus × paradisi, Grapefruit (Marsh, Star Ruby, Redblush, Chironja, Smooth Flat Seville)

Citrus × sinensis, Sweet Oranges (Blonde, Navel and Blood oranges)
Citrus amblycarpa 'Nasnaran' mandarin
Citrus depressa 'Shekwasha' mandarin
Citrus karna 'Karna', 'Khatta'
Citrus kinokuni 'Kishu mandarin'
Citrus lycopersicaeformis 'Kokni' or 'Monkey mandarin'
Citrus macrophylla 'Alemow'
Citrus reshni 'Cleopatra' mandarin
Citrus sunki (Citrus reticulata var. austera) Sour Mandarin
Citrus trifoliata (Poncirus trifoliata) Trifoliate Orange

The following mandarin cultivars are polyembryonic:
Dancy, Emperor, Empress, Fairchild, Kinnow, Mediterranean (Avana, Tardivo di Ciaculli), Naartje, Nova (Clemenvilla), Ortanique, Ponkan, Sampson, Satsumas (Hashimoto, Okitsu, Clausellina, Owari) Willowleaf.

The following lemon cultivars are polyembryonic:
Fino (Primofiori)
Verna (Berna)
Eureka
Lisbon

And a few more citrus types:
Marrakech limetta
Fukushu kumquat (Fortunella obovata)
Nanshôdaidai[6]

A SELECTION OF FRUITS THAT DO NOT GROW TRUE FROM SEED

Almond (Prunus amygdalus)
Apple (Malus spp.)
Avocado (Persea americana)
Banana (Musa spp.) N.B. Banana trees are really herbs.
Blueberry (Vaccinium spp.)
Cherry (Prunus cerasus)
Cherry Plum/Myrobalan Plum (Prunus cerasifera)
Currant - black, red and white - (Ribes spp.)
Fig (Ficus carica) N.B. figs are really flowers.
Gooseberry (Ribes spp.)
Grape (Vitis spp.)
Hazelnut (Corylus spp.)
Jaboticaba (Plinia cauliflora). Synonyms: Eugenia cauliflora, Eugenia jaboticaba, Myrcia jaboticaba, Myrciaria cauliflora, Myrciaria jaboticaba.) Hybrid or cultivar jaboticabas do not reproduce true from seed.
Jujube (Ziziphus jujuba)
Kiwi Fruit/Kiwi Berry (Actinidia spp.)
Loquat (Eriobotrya japonica)
Lucuma (Pouteria lucuma)
Macadamia (Macadamia spp.) Hybrid or cultivar macadamias do not come true from seed.
Mango (Mangifera spp.)
Mulberry (Morus spp.)
Naranjilla (Solanum quitoense)
Palm: (Arecaceae family) Edible palm fruits include dates, acai, Chilean Wine Palm fruit, Jelly Palm fruit and Peach Palm fruit.

Pear (Pyrus spp.)
Persimmon (Diospyros spp.)
Plum (Prunus domestica) other than greengage and damson.
Pomegranate (Punica granatum)
Raspberry (Rubus spp.)
Strawberry (Fragaria × ananassa) Hybrid or cultivar strawberries do not grow true from seed. The garden strawberry, has much larger fruit than the wild strawberry, but will not grow true from seed because it is a hybrid.

HIGHLY MONOEMBRYONIC CITRUS TYPES ...

... will produce seeds that will not come true to type. These include many 'true Citrus species' such as

> Ichang, Papeda (Citrus cavaleriei/Citrus ichangensis)
> Australian Desert Lime (Citrus glauca/Eremocitrus glauca)
> Indian wild orange (Citrus indica)
> Most kumquats (Citrus japonica/Fortunella) -
> Pummelo, Shaddock (Citrus maxima pomelo)
> Citron (Citrus medica)

And the citron hybrids:
> Persian Lime, Tahitian Lime, Bearss Lime (Citrus × latifolia)
> Bergamot Orange (Citrus × bergamia)

One true citrus species, the mandarin (Citrus reticulata), is highly variable. The following are monoembryonic:

> Clementines (Marisol, Oronules, Loretina, Beatriz, Clemenpons, Arrufatina, Esbal, Oroval, Clemenules, Orogrande, Tomatera, Fina, Nour, Hernandina, Clementard.)
> Ellendale
> Encore
> Fortune
> Fremont (50% monoembryonic)
> Temple
> Ugli
> Umatilla
> Wilking [7]

HOW TO OBTAIN SEEDS

Save seeds from your own garden plants or ask neighbours and friends for seeds from theirs. Buy fruit from your greengrocer or supermarket, or buy seeds from any reputable seed retailer. Check the use-by date on the packet.

HOW TO CLEAN SEEDS

If using seeds from fruit, remove the seed and wash off any fruit residue. The flesh surrounding the seed contains chemicals which actively prevent seed germination. Some seeds are small and numerous, such as guava seeds. To clean them, you need to place them in a ceramic dish, cover them with clean water and

---

[7]   *ibid*

leave them at room temperature for a week or more, to ferment. Periodically, place them in a fine mesh strainer and wash them under a running tap, stirring them with a metal spoon. Then return them to the ceramic dish, add some more clean water and gently swirl them around. Being heavier, the seeds will fall to the bottom, and much of the shredded, rotting flesh will float on the surface. Carefully tip out the floating detritus, leaving the seeds at the bottom. The seeds will not be clean the first time around and you will need to repeat this process until they are. Over time, this method ensures that the gradually disintegrating flesh is washed away.

SEED STORAGE

All seeds germinate more readily when fresh. Sow them as soon as possible. The fresher they are, the more viability they retain. Viability is the ability of the seed to germinate when it is given the right environmental conditions.

That said, sometimes, for whatever reason, you may have to keep seeds in storage for some time before planting. There are many seeds whose viability will last for years if they are properly stored; that is, kept dry and clean, protected from insects and in an environment with low temperatures, low humidity and low light levels.

'Store seeds in the refrigerator, not the freezer, until you are ready to plant them. A temperature of 10 degrees Celsius (50 degrees Fahrenheit) or less and 50 percent humidity or lower is ideal.

'If it is not practical to store seeds in your refrigerator, store them in any place that is cool, dark, and dry, protecting them from insects as much as possible.

As a general rule, store seeds in paper envelopes to allow air circulation and prevent mould from growing. You can, however, store them in plastic 'zip-lock' bags if they have been thoroughly air-dried. Label your seed packets, including date of collection and species name.

'Dusting the seeds with a mild insecticide will help prevent insect infestation and kill any pests collected with the seeds. Or, you can insert a pest strip for several days while leaving the paper bag open to allow insects to escape.' Some people use tomato dust for this purpose, because it contains compounds which are fungicidal, miticidal and insecticidal.

'Seeds of citrus and stone fruits should be kept moist to maintain viability. 'This type of seed should be planted immediately or mixed in a one-to-one ratio of moist sand, sphagnum moss or a peat and perlite mixture, and stored in a cool place. Citrus seeds will not live long even in the best storage conditions. If the root emerges from the seeds during storage, the seedling should be removed and planted immediately.

Apple seeds may be stored for several weeks, but they must be kept cool, dry and in darkness.

'Seed storage longevity varies from species to species. Some seeds may be viable after ten or more years of storage, while others may not germinate after two months in storage. Ideally, seeds should be planted within one year of collection'[8]

---

8 *Lady Bird Johnson Wildflower Center - The University of Texas at Austin, USA*

HOW TO PREPARE SEEDS FOR SOWING

A large number of plants use mechanisms to delay the germination of their seeds. We call this delay 'dormancy', from the Latin 'dormire', 'to sleep'. There are many reasons why a seed would want to remain asleep for a while before germinating. Here, we will only look at the seeds of plants that grow in temperate climates.

'The majority of plants ripen their seeds in late summer and early autumn when the weather is suitable for drying the seed. However, not many plants want their seed to germinate at that time of year since the small and vulnerable seedling would have to face the rigours of winter. Therefore various strategies are employed to delay germination until the spring. These strategies include:-

'A hard seed coat that slowly breaks down over winter and does not allow water to penetrate until late winter or spring (a seed cannot germinate until the embryo inside it has absorbed water).

'An immature embryo that does not ripen for some months after the seed has fallen.

'Assorted chemicals that inhibit germination. In nature, these are gradually leached out of the seed by rain.

'A sensitivity to cold. Some seeds require a period of cold weather in order for certain chemical changes to take place in the seed. Only after this cold spell can the seed germinate.

'Sometimes a period of warmth is also required and this can mean that the seed will not germinate until at least two winters have passed.

'Seeds often employ more than one of these strategies, which can complicate matters. Some seeds have so many inhibitory mechanisms that they may take four years or more to germinate.

'It is possible for the gardener just to sow the seed and sit back and wait for nature to take its course but, although this involves the least work it also has the greatest risks. The longer a seed is kept in a seedpod without germinating the more risk there is of the seed being lost either to insects, birds, mice, the gardener forgetting to water it in the summer and the seed desiccating and a whole host of other possible accidents. Plants produce thousands of seeds but only one seed during the entire lifetime of the parent plant has to come through to maturity in order to maintain the population, therefore in nature a huge loss is expected. Gardeners only get a few seeds and cannot afford to waste them. Therefore they look for ways to speed up the germination process.'[9]

SOWING 'GREEN' SEED

If the seed of certain species is harvested before it has fully dried the seed coat will not have fully developed and certain chemical inhibitors may not as yet have been put in the seed. By sowing the seed immediately it is harvested, usually in a cold frame[10] or outdoors, you can expect the seeds to germinate in the spring. This can save a year's wait and entails very little extra effort as long as the seed comes from your own plants. The trick is in judging when to harvest the seed. The embryo must be fully developed, or the

---

9   *Plants For a Future*
10   *A frame with a glass or plastic top in which small plants are grown and protected without artificial heat.*

seed will probably shrivel and die, but if you leave it too long to harvest the seed will have developed the various inhibitors. [11]

STRATIFICATION

'The pre-treatment of seeds (warm, cold, or variable stratification) is a simple measure used to break a seed's dormancy to enable the seed to germinate. By subjecting the seeds to the required pre-treatment, you are providing them with the natural effect that Mother Nature would have provided had the seeds been left to their natural course. By applying the required treatment yourself in a controlled environment such as a refrigerator, you can reduce factors that would have been detrimental to a seed had it been left to survive on its own in nature. By controlled stratification of the seeds, you are also able to control the time at which the seeds will germinate. By not stratifying the seeds that require this treatment, you will have to be content to accept nature's time frame, which could result in a delay of a year or more. Or, you may have no germination at all.

'Stratification[12] of seeds involves mixing the seed with a moist medium and keeping warm and/or cold for a certain time before sowing.'[13]

---

11   *Plants For a Future*
12   *The term 'stratification' is derived from the age old practice of stimulating seed to germinate by layering alternate strata of a moist media and seed. This media may be sand, vermiculite, perlite, peat, composted bark, sawdust, or potting media. The actual stratification involves placing the seed in this moist medium to simulate the natural conditions it would normally receive from its native environment. (Source: PFAF)*
13   *Plants For a Future*

TYPES OF STRATIFICATION

There are several types of stratification. Which type is proper for your seed depends on what that seed would normally experience in nature.

Warm-moist. Seeds from trees and shrubs that ripen their seeds in the early autumn usually require a warm moist treatment to induce germination. Temperature: 16 - 24 degrees C (62-75 degrees F). On top of your refrigerator is a good spot. Keep stratifying seeds out of the sun.

Cool-moist. Seeds that ripen in the late autumn or early winter generally require a cool moist treatment. This period of time is usually from one to four months. Temperature: 0 - 4 degrees C (32-40 degrees F). The vegetable compartment in your refrigerator is a good place.

Warm-moist-cool-warm. Depending on the species, some need a combination of warm and cool treatments followed by a warm period to germinate. Many seeds need one to four months of warm moist treatment, followed by cold treatment. In some, the root sprouts during the warm period, but the shoot does not sprout until after a cold period. These are sometimes called 'two-step' germinators. Some of these contain unformed embryos which must first develop at warm temperatures.

Some seeds are '70 - 40' germinators, which need warm moist, then cold moist, and germinate at cold temperatures.

Some tropicals which are slow to germinate (eg. many palms) need prolonged warmth to first develop their embryos.

Many seeds are 'multicycle' germinators, needing several cycles of cold and warm periods.

STRATIFYING YOUR SEEDS

To stratify your seeds, gather up all the necessary items before beginning. You will need:
* Your seeds
* Media. Medium grade vermiculite is recommended. You can also use a vermiculite-perlite mixture, sterile sand, or sterile milled sphagnum peat moss. If sawdust is used, it should be aged and not fresh.
* Water that has been boiled and cooled
* Waterproof pen (such as a Sharpie or Artline.)
* New, unused plastic zip-lock freezer bags
* Small plastic containers with tight fitting lids. Unless you are processing vast amounts of seed, these only need to be the size of about 4 matchboxes put together.
* Fungicide (optional)

Step 1: Sterilise
Rinse out the plastic containers with boiling water. Cleanliness is of the utmost importance when enclosing moist media in airtight containers. Fungus can thrive in these conditions. If the medium is not already sterile, you can place it in a microwave-safe dish and microwave it for 90 seconds per kilogram (2.2 pounds) on full power.

Step 2: Label.

Label the plastic bags with the waterproof pen. Include the stratification date started and when they are due to be removed from stratification. Some people also record the number of seeds.

Step 3: Scarify.

If (and only if) the seed has a hard case that requires mechanical scarification, follow the directions either on the seed packet or in this booklet.

Step 4: Soak.

A seed needs to begin absorbing moisture before it will sprout. Soak seeds in warm to hot (not boiling) water overnight before placing them into stratification unless otherwise instructed on the seed packet.

Step 5: Mix your stratification medium.

Add water to the medium. You may wish to mix in some fungicide at this point, but that is optional. The important thing is to have the vermiculite wet enough that it keeps the seeds moist but no so wet that the seeds are swimming in it. If they are too wet the seeds actually 'drown' from lack of air and if not wet enough they can't germinate.

Step 6: Place medium in containers.

With very clean hands, (or even wearing disposable plastic gloves) just gently squeeze the excess moisture out of the vermiculite. As a rule: you should not be able to squeeze any dripping water out of a handful of medium after thoroughly and uniformly moistening it. Do not squeeze vermiculite excessively hard as it will ruin the structure. When it's nicely damp, put some in the little plastic containers. Don't fill them more than half full.

Step 7: Add seeds.

With small containers, depending on the size of the seeds, it's best to put no more than about 16 in one container. This is so that if one seed gets fungus it won't affect too many others. Also they all need some room to themselves when they start sprouting. As a rule, use about 10 times the volume of medium to. seed volume. Close the lid tightly, and give the container a gentle shake to distribute the seeds through the medium and allow air to mix amongst the seeds and vermiculite. Place the container inside the labelled zip-lock bag.

Step 8: Stratify.

Make a note on your calendar of the date you placed your seeds into stratification and the date they should be removed. Put the sealed bags containing the sealed-containers into the proper cold or warm stratification environment.

Step 9: Follow-up.

Whenever you are stratifying seed, as the finishing time approaches check every week or two to see if germination is starting. When it does you will see white roots start to emerge from seeds, and if this happens then the seeds should be sown.

Note 1: Once stratification is started, a clock begins ticking in the seed and the shelf life begins to decrease. Seed should not stay in stratification for too long after its recommended stratification time, as it will use up its energy reserves and die.

Note 2: Some seeds that need cold stratification can be stubborn, and refuse to put forth a sprout even a couple of weeks after the due date. Often they will germinate if you subsequently put them into warm-stratification for a week or so and make them 'think' that spring has at last arrived.

Note 3: When checking your seeds do not prod them with your fingers. To investigate them, use a sterilised tool such as a metal teaspoon.

Step 10: Remove and Sow

Don't be overly concerned about exact lengths of pre-treatment time. After the required time period (or after 20% germination is noticed), remove the seeds and sow in flats or outside in the spring.[14]

SCARIFICATION

Scarification of seeds involves softening the hard seed coat in some way to allow water to soak into the seed. The simplest way of achieving this is to soak the seeds in hot water, allowing them to stand for several hours while the water cools. A second method is cool water soaking, washing or leaching. Alternatively, the seeds can be physically nicked or rubbed, eg. between two sheets of fine sandpaper.[15]

Scarified seeds do not store well and should be planted or stratified as soon as possible after treatment.

14	*Adapted from Plants For a Future*
15	*ibid.*

SCARIFYING WITH HOT WATER

Dipping: The seeds are dipped in boiling water for 10 seconds to 3 minutes. Produces erratic results, often killing many of the seeds and increasing fungal attack.

Warm soaking: Rarely used for heritage fruit seeds, this method is used mainly for legumes and is intended to speed up the germination rate by days rather than months. Water is brought to the boil and then allowed to cool very slightly. The best temperature is 88°C (190°F), but at least try to ensure the water is between 76 and 98 degrees Celsius (170 to 210 degrees Fahrenheit) and not boiling!

Pour a small amount of water onto the seed. Some growers use barely enough to cover the seed layer; others prefer to use at least 4 - 5 times the seeds' volume of water. You might wish to experiment.

This should then cool fairly rapidly. More hot water can be added a few minutes later, around the same as the quantity that was first added.

The hot water will soften the seed coat, leach out certain germination inhibitors that may be present and encourage the seed to absorb water. If the water is too hot it will kill the seeds.

Keep the container in a warm place for 12 - 24 hours while the seeds continue to soak. After that you can sow them.

Some seeds, such as those of acacia trees, will not germinate at all unless they are first soaked in very hot water. We mention acacias because many wattle trees have edible seeds and could be considered to be among Australia's indigenous heritage foods.

SCARIFYING WITH COLD WATER

This involves soaking, washing or leaching. Many seeds contain germination inhibitors which in nature prevent the seed from germinating except during the wet season (tropicals) or only after sufficient rain has fallen (desert plants). Soaking the seed in shallow water and changing every day for several days will leach out inhibitors. Heavy daily watering of pots may work. Some have oily coats and need detergent or peroxide soaks.[16]

SCARIFYING BY ABRASION

The cases of some seeds are hard and impermeable, and must be reduced by special means to allow moisture penetration, before the seed will germinate. In nature, this occurs as the seed is frozen in winter, or exposed to soil microbes that modify the seed coat. Scarification can also occur as seeds pass through the digestive tract of various birds and animals. Their stomach acids and gut enzymes soften the seed casing.

Man-made methods of scarification commonly used are mechanical, hot water, and acid. The best method is usually listed on packets of bought seeds.

Mechanical scarification, or abrasion, involves breaking, nicking, softening or weakening the seed coat with a file or sandpaper. The best results are from the least amount of nicking that will allow water to enter and the seed to swell. Many failures are due to over-abrading and damaging the seed. Different seeds need varying amounts of scarification.

Following the scarification, the seeds should be dull in appearance, but not deeply pitted or cracked as

---

16   *ibid*

to damage the embryo. Once scarified, seeds will not store well and should be planted as soon as possible after treatment. This treatment works well for larger seeds. Smaller seeds may be rubbed between sheets of 120 grit sandpaper. If the seeds are too small to see the progress, a different method such as soaking should be used.

Sandpaper or file Abrasion.

Reduce the seed coat by lightly rubbing it away with sandpaper or a file, or between two boards covered with sandpaper or any similar method, until just the very outer coat is scratched.

This works well with large seeds but is rather fiddly with small ones. You must be very careful not to file right through the seed coat and into the seed. You must be especially careful not to damage the embryo since this will kill the seed before it even germinates.

Sometimes you simply file one small area of the seed coat until you are almost through to the seed, at other times you may abrade the whole seed coat. This can be done by putting the seed into a lidded can that has a rough inner lining of sandpaper and then shaking the can for a while until the seed is abraded. It is very easy to overdo it if you are not careful.

De-waxing

Scarification by abrasion is also a good way of de-waxing. Some seeds are covered in a layer of wax (notably Myrica species such as Northern Bayberry) which stops the seeds absorbing water and germinating. This must be removed before stratification or sowing – the best way to do this is to rub the seeds between two sheets of coarse sandpaper (do it for periods of a few seconds at a time, then check the seeds — you only want to get rid of the wax and not damage the seeds!) Alternatively, seeds with a waxy coating may be washed several times in very hot water to remove the wax before the final soaking.

Nicking

Often, just scratching with a knife-point or scriber works. Other seeds need serious nicking, sometimes with a hacksaw until the white interior shows. Nicking seeds one by one can be tedious but is most effective. Alternatively, with some seeds it is sufficient to pierce the seed coat with a needle in order to admit water. Once again care must be taken not to damage the embryo.

Scarifying With Vinegar

Place seeds are placed in a glass (do not use any other type) container and covered with the proper concentration of vinegar. The concentration depends on the seed species. Stir the seeds gently with a glass rod and allow them to soak for 20 minutes to several hours, depending on the species. Ask your seed retailer about this - otherwise, there are reference books available which list proper soaking times. When the seed coat has been soaked for the proper amount of time, the seeds may be removed, washed, and stratified.

Combining Abrasion and Soaking

It is a good idea to rinse, then soak seeds in clean, room temperature water for several hours after you scarify them, to allow the water to penetrate to the embryo. Then plant the seed. [17]

---

17   *ibid*

OTHER METHODS OF GERMINATING SEEDS

DRY STORAGE OR AGEING

Many seeds will not germinate when freshly harvested, but are dormant until after a period of dry storage ranging from 1 - 12 months or up to 5 years. The time varies with temperature, humidity and oxygen. Often this type of dormancy can be broken with GA-3 (see below).

DRY HEAT

Certain types of seeds can be baked dry in an oven at 60° to 100°C (140° to 220°F) for 4 to 10 hours, or microwaved for 30 seconds to 4 minutes. This gives variable results.

SOAKING IN SPECIAL MEDIA

Soaking seed in potassium nitrate ($KNO3$), hydrogen peroxide, citric acid, sodium hypochlorite (bleach), smoke solution, charred wood leachate, gibberellic acid (GA3) or enzyme solutions have all been used to trigger germination of seeds. Some say that soaking seeds in malt extract or enzyme solutions works, too. Soaking seeds in liquid whey and apple cider vinegar mixed with water has also been used to help break dormancy.

Gibberellic acid-3 (Ga-3)

GA-3 is a naturally occurring plant growth regulator. Pre-soaking seeds in GA-3 will often cause rapid germination of many highly dormant seeds that would otherwise require cold, aging, light or other prolonged treatments. It can overcome many different types of dormancy. GA-3 is safe, easy to use, economical and rapidly becoming a standard tool for germinating seeds.

Smoke solution

Treatment with smoke essence in liquid form often helps germination of plants, particularly those from fire-prone environments such as California, Chile, Australia, South Africa, and the Mediterranean region. Either soak the seeds in this solution overnight (or until they swell), or water the pot or flat once with this solution.

You can buy commercially available smoke primers from garden centres, or mix your own, or make your own from scratch.

Smoke flavouring is found in the spice and flavouring or barbecue section of the grocery store . It comes in small brown bottles of liquid, called 'liquid smoke' or 'hickory seasoning'. Look for the 'all natural' type that lists only water and natural smoke concentrate as ingredients.

You may have to try different dilutions. To begin with, prepare a smoke solution by adding one part commercial smoke flavoring to nine parts water.

It is cheaper to make your own smoke primer. To do this, gather sticks of kindling wood, dried leaves (eucalyptus leaves work well), a fireproof bowl and a piece of metal screen to use as a grill. The screen should be wider than the pan. You can bend the screen into a slightly hollow shape so that seeds will not roll off into the fire and burn..

Pile the wood and leaves into the bowl and light them. Let the flames spread through the kindling. The aim is to create smoking embers, which will mimic bushfire smoke. Let the fire burn for 5 to 10 minutes, then blow out the flame, leaving only the smoking, charred twigs. Place the seeds on the screen, pick it up and wave the screen in the smoke. Continually test the smoke's temperature with your hand to make sure it is bearable. The goal is to smoke the seeds, not kill them. If it's very hot, move the screen further away from the embers.

Eucalyptus leaves ignite quickly and produce quantities of smoke. You can add extra leaves for more smoke as the fire smoulders. Smoke the seeds for 10 to 20 minutes, the longer the better, making sure they do not get too hot.

Finally, set aside the seeds and add water to the remains of the fire to capture the smoke essence. Let it soak. Break up any bigger pieces of charred wood by mashing them with a stick. When this burnt smoke-essence solution has cooled, combine it with your potting soil. Work it in, including even the charred twigs, which help to make the soil free draining. Plant the seeds in a sterile pot.

Another smoke treatment method is to burn a layer of straw or pine needles on top of the pot that has the seeds sown in it.

Hydrogen Peroxide

Soaking seeds in a 3% solution of food grade hydrogen peroxide for 10-30 minutes, followed by at least 10 rinses in clean water will kill most pathogens attached to the seed case.

Hydrogen peroxide is a biochemical stimulant of plant growth; a plant signalling molecule (like ethylene) used by plants to mediate pathogen and environmental stress responses. It also kills many plant pathogens. Staff members of plant research laboratories routinely soak seeds in dilute hydrogen peroxide in to prevent powdery mildew, mould damping off etc. It is important to use a very weak solution, otherwise you might kill the seed.

Charred Wood Leachate

Make your own by gathering a quantity of charred wood from your barbecue, home fire or bonfire. Place it in a container of clean water and let it stand for a few days, then strain out the solids. The water left behind is the leachate. It has percolated through the burnt wood and rinsed out some of the constituents. Like smoke solution, soaking in charred wood leachate tricks seeds into 'thinking' there has been a fire. After fires, the soil is clean, enriched, and bare of competing plants; it is a good time for seeds to germinate.

Potassium nitrate (KN03)

This chemical compound is also known as saltpetre. It is sometimes available from garden centres, though these days sales are strictly limited.

Citric acid

This is a baking aid which can be bought in most supermarkets.

Detergent

Seeds with oily coatings need to be washed in detergent.

Sodium hypochlorite

This is household bleach. Check the label to make sure the bleach does not have any other additives that might harm the seeds. Try using a 3% solution for soaking.

Note: Do not mix bleach and vinegar, as this produces a gas that can be detrimental to your health.

All seeds require different pre-sowing treatments, and it's best to find out which one suits the seeds you are sowing. Some need no treatment at all.

SOWING THE SEEDS

SOIL MIXES

'Many seeds do well sown direct to ordinary garden soil, but even good soil may be poor in pots or flats. These need a lighter, looser soil. Most commercial mixes are fine, but the addition of some garden soil and compost will often ensure adequate beneficial micro-organisms and fungi.

'A good soil mix can be made at home from 1/3 garden loam, 1/3 peat or compost, and 1/3 gritty sand. Crushed charcoal also helps.'

SOWING AND GROWING

'When the time has come to sow after pre-treatment, you have a choice of planting direct into nursery beds in the garden or into flats. Nursery beds should be shaded in the afternoon and be weed-seed free. The soil should also be friable with lots of organic matter and not prone to crusting over after a rain.

'Seeds which take a long time to germinate are best sown in seed trays or pots, and covered with sand rather than compost. Very small seeds should be sown on the surface of the compost and the tray/pot kept moist by enclosing it in a plastic bag.

'If planting in pots, your seed-starting mix should be evenly moist, but not soaking wet. Do not sow the seeds too thickly, as this can lead to poor air circulation and 'damping off' problems.

'You don't have to separate the stratification medium from the seeds. Spread the seed mixture over the surface of the soil in the flat or pot and cover it with a thin layer of fine perlite or sand. After planting, immediately water in the seed and thereafter keep the soil properly moistened but not soaking wet.

'After germination, provide good air circulation and do not let the seedlings dry out. Watering from the bottom will help to prevent fungal diseases from forming on the surface.

'Once the seedlings have developed their first set of true leaves, transplant to larger pots or nursery beds. Do not allow them to become pot bound.

AFTERCARE

'Watering is the main thing to be aware of once the seed is sown. The compost must not be allowed to dry out, but neither must it be sodden. The seed, especially as it starts to germinate, is very susceptible to drought or waterlogging and easily killed by either.'[18]

USEFUL TIPS

Water your seedlings with a weak seaweed solution. Seaweed is a natural plant tonic which improves the root system.

---

18   *Plants For a Future*

If you're growing your seedlings indoors, beside a window or under lights, watch out for tiny fungus gnats. A few will not do much harm but a heavy infestation can cause root damage. To control fungus gnats mix a few drops of soil-wetting solution or pure, grey-water-safe dishwashing liquid into the water you use for your seedlings.

'Getting the seed to germinate is only the start of course. Now you must look after the young seedlings so that they will eventually become mature plants.

'Finally, don't give up if seeds don't germinate, or only a few germinate, in the first year - many seeds spread out their germination over more than one year.[19]

---

19   ibid.

WHICH METHOD FOR WHICH SEED?

'Having learnt the various methods of inducing seed to germinate, how can you tell which method(s) to apply to the seed of any particular species?'[20]

A great deal of useful information is available online, particularly at the Plants For a Future Database, but you can also work out a seed's probable needs by knowing something about its native habitat.

'One very simple rule of thumb for growing trees, shrubs and other perennials from areas with cold winters is that, if in doubt, sow the seed as soon as it is ripe.

'If the plants you want to grow come from areas with milder winters (with only occasional frosts) then sowing the seed in late winter is usually more appropriate.

'If the plants come from areas that experience no frosts, then sowing the seed in mid spring is usually best.

'If the seed of any species that you obtain has a hard seedcoat, then it cannot do any harm if you scarify it using any of the methods mentioned above.'[21]

Agroforestry U.K. give these examples of pre-sowing treatments for different types of seeds:

ND - Not dormant, sow in spring.
SI - Not dormant, but must be sown immediately.
SC - Scarify and sow in spring.
CS - Cold stratify. Followed by a number of weeks, eg. CS 13 = cold stratify 13 weeks (3 months).
WS - Warm stratify. Followed by a number of weeks, eg. WS 6 = warm stratify 6 weeks.

---
20   *Plants For a Future*
21   *ibid*

GERMINATING SPECIFIC SEEDS

Almonds (Prunus dulcis)
Seed requires 2 - 3 months cold-moist stratification and is best sown as soon as it germinates. Stored seed can be slow, sometimes taking 18 months to germinate.

Apple (Malus spp.)
No scarification or soaking necessary. Cold-moist stratify for 6 - 16 weeks or even longer, until you see the seed cases split and a white root beginning to sprout. If the seeds appear to be still dormant after eight weeks plant them any way and there's a good chance they will germinate. Plant them very close to the top of the soil - they need light to show them which direction to drive their roots into the soil and which direction to push up their leaves.

Bayberry (Myrica spp.)
Seed - best sown as soon as it is ripe in the autumn in a cold frame. Barely cover the seed and keep it moist.
Dewax+CS13+SC Stored seed germinates more freely if dewaxed, then cold stratified for 13 weeks, then scarified before planting; see instructions above.

Bilberry, Whortleberry (Vaccinium myrtillus)
Stratification: CS16

Blackberries & other Briar Berries (Rubus spp.)
Blackberry seed requires cold stratification for one to six months before being planted. The average is approximately three months. Alternatively you can

plant them outdoors early in autumn and let the seed embryos mature naturally through winter. Commercial varieties of blackberries are commonly propagated by root cuttings or tip layering.
Note: blackberries are a weed of national significance in Australia.

Black Mulberry (Morus nigra)
Stratification: CS16

Black Walnut (Juglans nigra)
Cold stratification for 90 to 120 days is required for optimum seed germination but the necessity and duration of stratification may vary by seed source. Seeds should be planted in autumn in moist, well-drained, deep soil that is rich in organic matter. Black walnut prefers full sun.

Cherimoya (Annona spp.)
SI. Sow fresh. Can be stored for up to two weeks if kept moist.

Cherry (Prunus spp.)
'Various cultivars of cherry differ somewhat in their cold stratification requirements. Some need only about four weeks while others require as long as 14 or more weeks under the same conditions. The seeds germinate, and the seedlings grow freely at a temperature close to freezing; therefore, while in stratification, cherry seed must be under frequent observation, particularly during the last part of the recommended stratification period.'[22]

---

[22] *How to Propagate from Seed. B. Dean McCraw.*

Cherry Plum, Myrobalan. (Prunus cerasifera)
Stratification: WS4+CS20

Citrus
'Some seeds (such as citrus) are 'borderline' desiccation-intolerant. These can be dried and stored for some time, but lose viability quickly and germinate slowly once they've been dried. Slow germination rates and lowered viability make borderline desiccation-intolerant seeds susceptible to damping-off or other microbial damage during germination. For this reason even seeds which are only borderline desiccation-intolerant perform best if planted fresh.' [23]

Citrus seeds can often take several weeks to germinate, so be patient.

Cornelian Cherry (Cornus mas)
Stratification: CS23

Culinary Myrtle (Myrtus communis)
Stratification: ND

Date Plum (Diospyros lotus)
Stratification: CS4

Elderberry (Sambucus nigra)
Stratification: WS13+CS26

Feijoa/Pineapple Guava (Acca sellowiana syn. Feijoa sellowiana)
Stratification: ND

---

23   *Vegetable Seed Saving Handbook, Jack Rowe.*

Grape (Vitis spp.)
Grape seed requires cold stratification, varying in length from 90 to 140 days.
Commercial varieties of grapes are propagated by cuttings and grafting and sometimes by budding and layering.

Guava (Psidium spp,)
Eg. Strawberry guava (Psidium cattleianum) and yellow cherry guava cattleianum littorale). Sow seeds as soon as fruit is ripe, after cleaning off the flesh. In warm climates these seeds require no stratification but we have found that when planted outdoors in the cooler southern states they naturally lapse into dormancy over winter and germinate in spring.
If planting stored seed, abrade the hard outer shell (see above) to increase germination chances.

Hardy Kiwi Fruit. (Actinidia arguta)
Stratification: CS13

Hazelnuts (Cobnuts/Filberts) Corylus spp.
These are best sown when fresh. They will acquire a deep embryonic dormancy if the seed is allowed to dry out. Best chances of some germination of stored seed follow 2 - 6 months of stratification (moist chill of 40F).

Hickories, Pecans (Carya spp.)
Stratification: CS12 or plant outside in autumn.

Jaboticaba (Plinia or Eugenia spp.)
Sow fresh. Can be stored for up to two weeks if kept moist.

Japanese Raisin Tree (Hovenia dulcis)
Stratification: SC

Melon & Watermelon (Cucumis & Citrullus spp.)
Sow them directly into the ground in spring. Melon seeds can be cleaned, dried and stored for up to two years in labelled plastic zip-lock bags in the refrigerator.

Passionfruit Passiflora edulis
The seed is best sown when fresh. Old, stored seed can take months germinate. Buy some passionfruit, separate half a dozen seeds from the pulp, and plant them as soon as possible. Fresh seed may take ten to twenty days to germinate.
'The best way seems to be to just put them in the garden and leave them be, and eventually they come up. Or not.
'Seeds of hybrid varieties do not grow true to type. If you live in a cooler climate the passionfruit you buy may be a hybrid variety. If you grow that seed you don't know what you'll get. To be more certain of the result, find out the identity of the fruit you buy, or buy commercial seed.
'One reason for not growing passionfruit from seed is the high susceptibility of the purple varieties and the hybrids to the root disease 'fusarium wilt'. There are resistant root stocks (flavicarpa varieties). If Fusarium wilt is a problem in your soil, and if you need to grow susceptible varieties because of your cool climate, then you may prefer to invest in a grafted plant from a nursery.'[24]

---

24   Tropical Permaculture Gardens

European Pear (Pyrus spp.)
Same as apple. Stratification: CS16

Peach, Nectarine and Apricot.
(Prunus persica, Prunus persica var nucipersica and Prunus armeniaca.)
The pits, or seeds, of ripe stone-fruits will not germinate straight away but require 90 days of cold stratification. To stratify stone fruit seeds artificially, first soak them in cool water for 24 hours, then follow the instructions for cold stratification, above.

'As soon as sprouting begins, the seed should be planted or stored at a lower temperature 0°C to 0.5°C (32° to 33° F) until planting is possible.

'Germinating seed must be planted carefully, as the young sprouts are brittle and easily broken. It is not necessary to separate the mix from the seed when planting. Peaches should be sown about one and one-half inches deep.'[25]

To stratify stone-fruit seeds naturally, simply clean off any remaining fruit pulp and plant them outdoors in autumn. Of course, this method only works in cool and temperate climates, such as exist in the southern Australian states.

Persimmon (Diospyros virginiana)
'Propagation of persimmon is difficult and germination of its seed uncertain. Stratification at a low temperature (0°C to 2°C) for a period of 20 to 40 days, or autumn planting of unstratified seed has

---

25   Seed Germination for Rootstocks. University of Georgia Department of Entomology

been reported effective in breaking dormancy and forcing germination.'[26]

Plum (Prunus spp.)
'Plum seed requires cold stratification. The exact period for plums varies with the cultivar. It's usually about 60 to 90 days. Plum seed germinates freely at a low temperature once the after-ripening is completed. Therefore, make periodic observations of stratified seed and lower the temperature if germination starts too soon.'[27]

Salal, Shallon (Gautheria shallon)
CS17

Saskatoon, Serviceberry, Juneberry etc. (Amelanchier spp.)
This is best harvested 'green', when the seed is fully formed but before the seed coat has hardened, and then sown immediately in pots outdoors or in a cold frame. If you wish to germinate stored seed, follow this procedure if starting seed artificially:
Scarification: Soak in water, let stand in water for 24 hours.
Stratification: warm stratify for 60 days, cold stratify for 90 days.
Germination: sow seed 1cm deep, tamp the soil, and mulch the seed bed. To germinate amelanchier seed naturally, sow it in

---

[26] B. Dean McCraw, *Extension Tree Fruit and Pecan Specialist. Based on original material prepared by E. L. Whitehead, Oklahoma State University Extension Service.*
[27] ibid

summer in mulched beds. It should germinate the following spring.

When the seedlings are large enough to handle, prick them out into individual pots and grow them on in a sheltered outdoor position, planting them out once they are 20cm or more tall. Grow the seedlings on for two years in the seedbed before planting them out into their permanent positions during the winter.

Sea Buckthorn (Hippophae rhamnoides)
Stratification: CS17

Service Tree/Checker Tree (Sorbus domestica)
Stratification: CS17

Smooth Kiwi Fruit (Actinidia chinensis)
Stratification: CS4

Stone Pine, Umbrella Pine, Italian Stone Pine (Pinus pinea) Stratification: CS0-4

Wild Strawberry/Woodland Strawberry/Alpine Strawberry (Fragaria vesca)
Stratification: CS4

Suckers

Varieties of fruit trees and shrubs are perpetuated and increased by the removal of a portion of the plant, and making it by various means into a new one. In some cases this is done by means of suckers, which are shoots that many kinds of trees and shrubs send up from the roots or underground stems.

Suckers of some trees, and more particularly Pears, Quinces, Plums, and Cherries, are frequently used as stocks for budding and grafting, but they are, generally speaking, less vigorous than seedlings, and retain the tendency of their parents to throw up shoots from their roots.

Figs are often propagated by removing the suckers and planting them out direct. The usual method of propagating Raspberries is also by suckers, which form the canes.

The runners of Strawberries are simply overground suckers, which have power to form perfect plants.

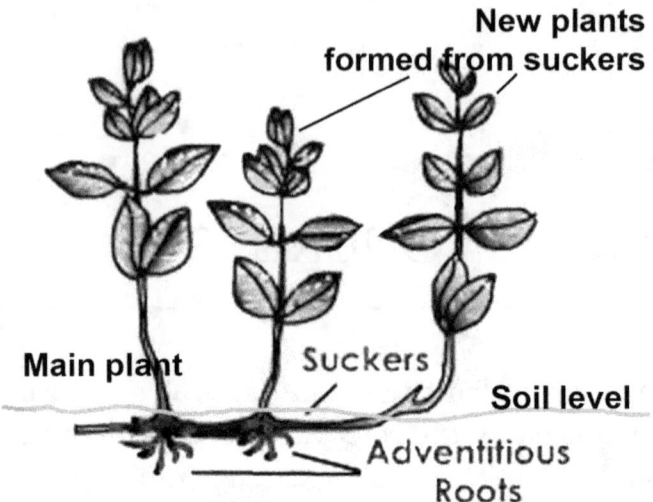

LAYERS

This method of propagation is sometimes adopted, but it is open to the objection that the plants are less vigorous and thriving than seedlings. Sometimes it is employed for raising blight-proof[1] and dwarfing stocks for the Apple, and the Olive is often increased by this method.

Layers are simply cuttings that are rooted without being separated from the parent plants. The operation is readily performed, all that is necessary being to bend down the branches and insert a portion 7 or 10 cm (3 or 4 inches) deep in the ground, leaving the end above the surface.

The rooting of the branch will be facilitated by cutting a notch just below a bud on the buried part, or making a slit upwards from 2 to 5 cm (1 to 2 inches) in length. Hooked pegs are generally used to keep the branches in their places, and in fixing the earth care should be taken that the slit portion is kept open to some extent.

---

1   Note: At least until 2013, Australia was fortunate enough to be free of fire-blight.

LAYERING.

 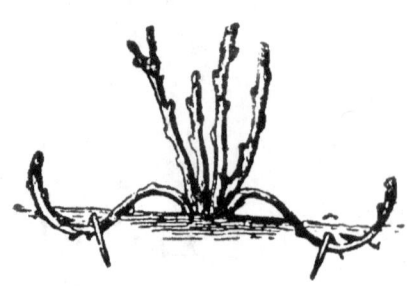

Crook for pegging down layers.   Shrub layered by covering the shoots and pegging them down.

Deciduous trees may be layered at any time after the fall of the leaf, but the best time is just before active growth commences in the spring. Evergreens may be layered at various times, but the most favourable period is early in the autumn.

HILLOCK LAYERING

What is called Hillock layering is practised by some growers, and more especially with dwarf Apples, the Fig, Quince, and Hazelnut.

When this practice is adopted, the stocks are cut back close to the ground in spring, or early summer, and a mound of earth 15 or 20 cm (6 or 8 inches) deep is placed over the stump. Young stems will start, and form roots, and in the following autumn or winter these plants should be separated from the parent stems. Trees treated in this way may be layered yearly.

Growers of apple rootstocks often use this method.

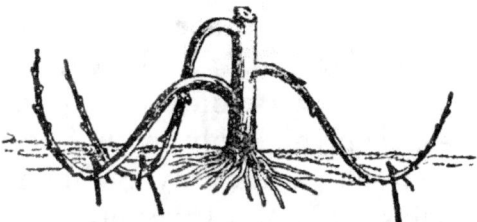

Tree layered with notched branches to facilitate the formation of roots.

Layer with a ring of bark removed from one branch (*A*), and a slit in the other (*B*); either practice facilitates rooting.

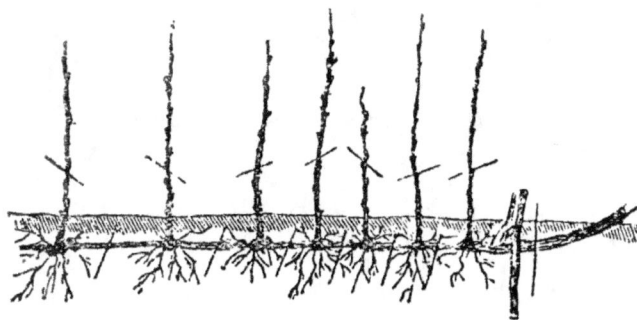

Layer of grape vine with branch entirely covered, making a plant at every joint. Cross marks showing where the young plants should be cut back at the first pruning.

AIR LAYERING

Air layering is a method of propagation that allows new roots to grow from an aerial branch that is still attached to the parent tree. It is also called marcotting.

First you use a sharp knife to cut into the bark of the parent tree, then you apply rooting hormone to the cut. Wrap the cut with a thick layer of damp sphagnum moss, then enclose this in a thick layer of plastic film to keep the mixture in. Tie the bundle together firmly and leave it for several months. When sufficient roots have grown from the wound, cut the branch off the parent tree and plant it.

Air layering. Image: www.fao.org

Cuttings

All fruit trees and shrubs may be propagated by cuttings, and some kinds are commonly raised by this method, such as the Grape, Currant, Gooseberry, Fig, Hazel, Mulberry, and Quince. Good plants of all these fruits may be obtained from cuttings, but in the case of other kinds growth is too slow and weakly to allow this method to be utilized. In fact, excepting the kinds named, cuttings will never make vigorous and thriving plants.

Cuttings of Gooseberries and Currants should be taken off when the plants are pruned, leaving them about 30 cm (12 inches) long, making the base just below a bud, with as clean a cut as possible. The cuttings should be inserted about half their depth in the ground, and all buds below the surface, except the two lower ones, ought to be removed, in order to check the tendency to form suckers. The cuttings may be planted at any time before the spring, but it is advisable to get them in earlier than other fruits, because growth becomes active sooner.

Grape cuttings should be made from 25 to 38 cm (10 to 15 inches) long, with four or five joints, and ought to be planted about half their depth in the ground.

1. Ordinary cutting of the previous season's wood. Cross line showing the depth it should be planted.
2. Cutting with a heel or small portion of two year old wood attached.
3. Mallet cutting with a solid piece of two year old wood attached.

They should be selected from well-ripened wood of the previous season's growth, and shoots that have home fruit. The very best cuttings are those taken from the lower part of the shoots, and if they can be taken off with a piece of the old wood attached, or what is technically called a heel, they will root with greater facility. It is not advisable to plant Grape cuttings early, as they generally make a better start if put in after spring has commenced.

Figs and Hazel nuts may be readily propagated from cuttings of the last season's wood, from 25 to 38 cm (10 to 15 inches) long, preparing and planting them as recommended for the Grape. Most trees propagate most readily from cuttings of the previous season's growth, but they may be formed from older wood in some cases.

The Mulberry and Olive will strike freely from wood of various ages, and large branches may be rooted without difficulty. Though cuttings may be struck when planted out where the trees are to remain, yet the safer plan is to set them in nursery beds, where the cultivator can give them the necessary care and attention till they are rooted. Though in the case of a vineyard this practice will entail a little more labour, yet the chances of rooting the plants will be much better

SUITABLE SHOOT FOR MAKING A CUTTING.

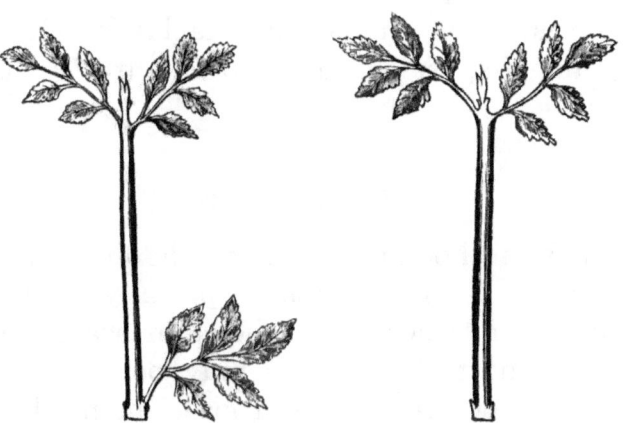

CUTTING PARTLY PREPARED.   SOFT-WOODED CUTTING READY FOR INSERTING.

Complaints are often made that cuttings, and more especially those of the Grape, fail to root freely; but this is in most cases due to causes that the grower can control. Sometimes the cuttings are allowed to get dried too much from exposure before they are planted, when, as a matter of course, their vigour is impaired. Then, again, they often perish through the land becoming sodden, or from its getting dried up.

The greatest care should be taken to protect all shoots intended for cuttings from exposure to atmospheric influences [too much wind, sun or frost] after they are separated from the parent plants. Much injury is often the result of this exposure, and as a rule all cuttings, or wood intended for them, should be wholly or partially covered with moist soil or sand till required for planting.

The rooting of all cuttings will be greatly facilitated by placing a layer of broken charcoal, say about an inch deep, underneath. Let the charcoal be broken to the size of peas and under, and let the heels of the cuttings rest upon the top of the layer. The writer, from a long experience, can confidently recommend this plan.

EYE-CUTTINGS

This is a method of propagation adopted with some fruit-bearing plants, and more especially the Grape. It is serviceable for increasing choice or scarce varieties of Grapes quickly, as plants may be obtained from every bud; but for ordinary purposes the method offers no particular advantages.

This method uses pieces of foliated or defoliated stalks with one or more eyes. Single-eye cuttings can be taken from plants that have alternate leaves, allowing one axillary bud per cutting. Double-eye cuttings are taken from plants that have opposite leaves, leaving two leaves and buds per cutting.

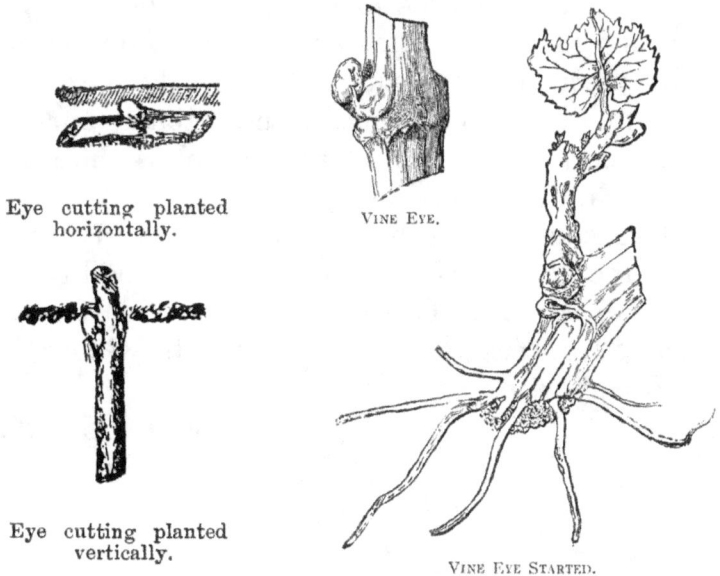

Eye cutting planted horizontally.

Vine Eye.

Eye cutting planted vertically.

Vine Eye Started.

When this mode of propagation is practised, plump well-formed buds should be selected, with about 5cm (a couple of inches) of the wood below and 1 cm (half-an-inch) above the eye attached. These eye-cuttings should be either planted horizontally in sand or light soil, about two inches below the surface, pressing the earth rather firmly about them; or they may be placed vertically with the eye a little below surface level. The best time for planting is just as growth is commencing in the spring, and rooting will be facilitated if the cuttings can be placed in a hotbed, which will supply a steady bottom heat.

ROOT-CUTTINGS

Some kinds of fruit trees and shrubs can be readily propagated, by pieces of the roots, and this mode of increasing stocks is often serviceable. For the purpose, fleshy pieces of the roots must be taken from 5 to 10 cm (2 to 4 inches) in length, and in early spring these should be planted about an inch below the surface in sand or light soil.

If placed in a hotbed, with a steady bottom heat, these root cuttings will strike more readily than in the open ground. This mode of propagation is often practised successfully with Currants, Goose berries, and Raspberries.

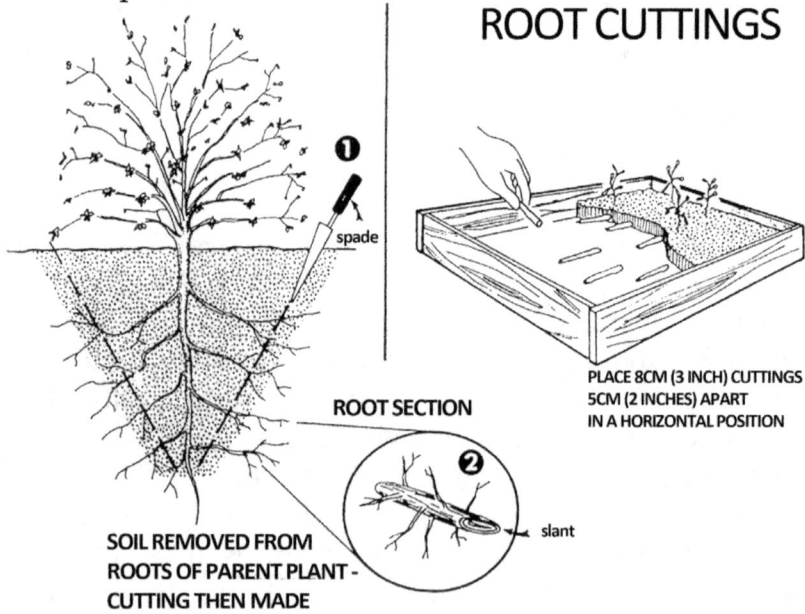

Image: Agriscience, MSU

DIVISION

Dividing the parent plant is one of the easiest ways to propagate many small fruits. By the time a berry bush is several years old, new plants usually have started to form around the original one. If you want to start as many new little bushes as possible, the best way is to dig up the entire plant and split it with your axe, knife, or pruning shears. Just make sure, before you cut, that each division will have a good clump of roots on it.

If you want only two or three new plants, you can sometimes sever them from their parent with a quick thrust of a sharp shovel without greatly disturbing the main plant.

The best time to make divisions is in early spring just as new growth starts, or just prior. The brambles (raspberries and blackberries) are especially easy to divide.

STOOLING

Some bush fruits — currants, elderberries, and gooseberries, for instance — can be started by dividing the large plants. Blueberries can also be divided, but, except for the lowbush kinds, they do not form offsets as easily. You can get the bush fruits to produce large numbers of new plants by cutting back the top of the bush to about 6 inches in height, and piling rich soil or compost over it, completely covering it. New shoots will grow through the soil, and roots will form on their stems. Replace any soil that may wash away in rains, and, the following spring, dig up the entire plant, cut the new plants apart, and transplant them. This process is called 'stooling' the plant.

RÖDA VINBÄR, RIBES RUBRUM L.

BIBLIOGRAPHY

About.com. *Gardening* (2013)

Agroforestry Research Trust U.K. *Seed List And Order Form* with stratification information, (2013)

Crichton, David Alexander. *The Australasian Fruit Culturist.* (1893)

Davis, Walter. *Plant Propagation* (1922)

Fruit and Nut Research & Information Center, University of California, (2013)

Koskinen, Jorma. *Citrus Pages* (2013)

Lady Bird Johnson Wildflower Center, The University of Texas at Austin, USA

Lloyd, John and Mitchinson, John. *QI: The Complete First Series – QI Factoids.* (2006).

McClendon, Tom. *Hardy Citrus for the South East* Southeastern Palm Society (SPS Publishing).

McCraw, B. Dean *How to Propagate Fruits And Nuts By Seed.* Based on original material prepared by E.

L. Whitehead, Oklahoma State University Extension Service.

Michigan Agriscience and Natural Resources Education, USA. *Sexual And Asexual Reproduction* (2013)

Plants For a Future database, www.pfaf.org

Rowe, Jack. Vegetable Seed Saving Handbook.

Seeds of Change. *Frequently Asked Questions* (2013)

Stirzaker, Richard. *Out of the Scientist's Garden: A Story of Water and Food.* Collingwood, VIC: CSIRO Pub. (2010).

Tropical Permaculture Gardens (2013)

University of Georgia Department of Entomology. *Seed Germination for Rootstocks*

Vegetative Propagation Food and Agriculture Organization of the United Nations. (2013)

Wikipedia (2013)

GLOSSARY

Plant breeding: the application of genetic principles to produce plants that are more useful to humans. This is accomplished by selecting plants found to be economically or aesthetically desirable, first by controlling the mating of selected individuals, and then by selecting certain individuals among the progeny. Such processes, repeated over many generations, can change the hereditary makeup and value of a plant population far beyond the natural limits of previously existing populations[1].

Rootstock: A plant with roots, onto which another variety is grafted.

Flat: A shallow frame or box for seeds or seedlings.

Open-pollinated seeds: These are produced from a population of 'parent' plants with very similar genetic characteristics. Open-pollinated plants, grown in isolation to prevent cross-pollination with another variety of the same species, will produce offspring that are very similar to the original parent population, allowing seeds to be saved and grown

---

[1] *Encyclopedia Britannica*

out 'true-to-type' year after year, generation after generation. These varieties can also be selected for disease resistance.[2]

Heirloom seeds: These are open-pollinated varieties that have been maintained and handed down by seed savers for at least 60 years.

F1 hybrid seeds: These are the first generation of offspring plants produced by a cross of two genetically different parent varieties, usually of the same species. (F1 is short for Filial 1, meaning 'first offspring'). Hybrids can have advantages, including robust growth known as 'hybrid vigor,' uniformity, and the fact that they are often bred to be disease resistant. Since the 1920s, many hybrid varieties have been bred using traditional breeding methods. Seed saved from F1 Hybrids will not grow 'true-to-type'.[3]

GMO seeds: GMO stands for 'genetically modified organism'. More accurately, these are the seeds of cultivars created using 'recombinant DNA technology'. They can be either hybrids or open pollinated varieties. Recombinant DNA technology is the ability to combine DNA molecules from different sources into one molecule in a test tube. The inserted DNA may come from related or unrelated species, or created in a laboratory. GMOs are not permitted in organic farming systems.[4]

---

2   *Seeds of Change*
3   *ibid*
4   *ibid*

INDEX

A

air layering 50
almond 12, 37
apple 5, 12, 37, 47, 48
avocado 12

B

banana 12
Berries and Small Fruits
  alpine strawberry 10, 44
  bayberry 9, 37
  bilberry 37
  blackberry 9, 37
  black mulberry 12, 38
  blueberry 12
  Brazilian Cherry 9
  briar berries 37
  Ceylon Hill Gooseberry 9
  Cornelian Cherry 39
  elderberry 39
  gooseberry 12
  juneberry 10, 43
  raspberry 13, 45
  saskatoon 10, 43
  serviceberry 43
  strawberry 13, 45
  whortleberry 37
  wild strawberry 10
  woodland strawberry 10
biodiversity xx
black walnut 10, 38

C

charred wood leachate 32
checker tree 44
cherimoya 9, 38
cherry 12
Cherry of the Rio Grande 9

Citrus 4, 16, 39
  alemow 11
  Australian Desert Lime 13
  bergamot 13
  calamondin 10
  citrange 10
  citron 13
  clementines 14
  'Cleopatra' mandarin 11
  fukushu kumquat 11
  grapefruit 5
  grapefruit 10
  ichang papeda 13

Indian Sweet Lime 10
karna 11
key lime 10
kishu mandarin 11
kumquat 13
lemon 5, 11
mandarin 5, 14, 11
Marrakech limetta 11
Mexican Lime 10
monkey mandarin 11
nanshôdaidai 11
nasnaran' mandarin 11
oranges 5
Otaheite Lime 10
Palestine Lime 10
pummelo 13
Rangpur Lime 10
rough lemon 5, 10
shekwasha mandarin 11
sour mandarin 11
sour orange 5
sweet oranges 10
Tahitian Lime 13
trifoliate orange 5
trifoliate orange 11
West Indian Lime 10
Crichton, David Alexander 1
cross-pollination 6
culinary myrtle 39
cultivar ix, 7
currant 12
custard apple 9
cuttings 51

D

date plum 39
de-waxing 27
division 57
dormancy 17
dragon fruit 9

E

eye-cuttings 54

F

feijoa 9, 40
fig 12, 45, 48
fire blight xviii

G

germinating seeds 29, 37
gibberellic acid-3 29
Granny Smith xi
grape 12, 40
guava 9, 40

H

hardy kiwi fruit 40
hazelnut 12, 40, 48
heritage fruit ix, x, xx, 7
heterozygotes 3, 8
hickories 41
hillock layering 48
homozygotes 4, 7

I

Italian Stone Pine 9, 44

J

jaboticaba 9, 12, 41
japanese raisin tree 41
jujube 12

K

kiwi berry 12
kiwi fruit 12

L

layers 47
loquat 12
lucuma 12

M

macadamia 9, 12
mango 12
melon 9, 41

N

naranjilla 12

O

olive 47, 52
open-pollinated 6

P

palm 12
passionfruit 9, 41
pear 5, 12, 42, 45
pecan 41
persimmon 13, 43
pineapple guava 40
pitaya 9
pleach xiii
pomegranate 13
preparing seeds for sowing 17

Q

quince 9, 45, 48

R

root-cuttings 56
rootstock 8, 48

S

salal 43
scarification 24
sea buckthorn 44
seeds 3, 14
seed storage 15
service tree 44
shallon 43
smoke solution 30
smooth kiwi fruit 44
soil mixes 33
sowing 'green' seed 18
Stone Fruit 16
  apricot 5, 9, 42
  cherry 12, 38, 45
  cherry plum 12, 39
  damson plum 9
  greengage plum 9
  myrobalan plum 12, 39
  nectarine 9, 42
  peach 5, 9, 42
  plum 13, 43, 45
stone pine 9, 44
stooling 57
stratification 19
stratification 44
suckers 45
Surinam Cherry 9
sweet chestnut 10

T

tamarillo 10
tomatillo 10
tomato 10
true to type 3

U

umbrella pine 44

V

virus 7
viruses 5

W

watermelon 6, 10, 41
wild strawberry 44
woodland strawberry 44

Some Heritage Fruit Groups in Australia

Werribee Park Heritage Orchard, situated near Melbourne, Australia, is a beautiful antique orchard dating from the 1870s, on the grounds of the old mansion by the Werribee River. It was renowned for its peaches, grapes, apples, quinces, pears, a variety of plums and several other fruits, as well as walnuts and olives. Recently this historic treasure has been rediscovered. Volunteers are replanting and tending the orchard.
www.werribeeparkheritageorchard.org.au

The Heritage Fruits Society is also based in Melbourne, Australia. Their aim is to conserve heritage fruit varieties on private and public land. They enable and encourage society members to research this wide range of varieties and to inform the public on the benefits of heritage fruits for health, sustainability and biodiversity.
www.heritagefruitssociety.org.au

The Heritage and Rare Fruit Network's purpose is to provide a forum for sharing information on all varieties of fruit and less common useful plants, to link up people with an interest in growing unusual fruit, and to support sharing of propagation material through grafting days and any other means.
heritageandrarefruits.weebly.com

The Rare Fruit Society of South Australia is an amateur organisation of fruit tree growers who preserve heritage varieties, explore climate limitations and study propagation, pruning and grafting techniques.
www.rarefruit-sa.org.au

www.ingramcontent.com/pod-product-compliance
Lightning Source LLC
LaVergne TN
LVHW051509070426
835507LV00022B/3014